50 Party Recipes Everyone Will Love

By: Kelly Johnson

Table of Contents

- Crispy Chicken Wings
- Mini Beef Sliders
- Loaded Nachos
- Classic Deviled Eggs
- Veggie Spring Rolls
- Stuffed Mushrooms
- Guacamole and Chips
- Spinach and Artichoke Dip
- Meatball Sliders
- Caprese Skewers
- Buffalo Cauliflower Bites
- Shrimp Cocktail
- Cheese and Charcuterie Board
- Pigs in a Blanket
- Baked Brie with Jam
- Mini Quiches
- Hummus with Pita and Veggies
- Guacamole-Stuffed Peppers
- Bacon-Wrapped Dates
- Jalapeño Poppers
- Chicken Satay with Peanut Sauce
- Spinach and Cheese Stuffed Pretzels
- Shrimp and Avocado Crostini
- Mini Tacos
- Cheese-Stuffed Breadsticks
- Sweet and Sour Meatballs
- Bruschetta with Tomato and Basil
- Mozzarella Sticks
- Sweet Potato Fries with Dip
- Mini Caprese Bites
- Loaded Potato Skins
- Stuffed Jalapeños
- Cucumber Bites with Cream Cheese
- Pulled Pork Sliders
- Veggie Platter with Dip

- Meat and Cheese Empanadas
- Popcorn Chicken
- Fruit and Cheese Skewers
- Shrimp Spring Rolls
- Cheddar and Bacon Biscuits
- Parmesan Zucchini Fries
- Tzatziki with Fresh Veggies
- Beef Empanadas
- Taco Dip
- Bruschetta with Goat Cheese
- Caprese Salad Bites
- Crab Cakes with Remoulade
- Guacamole and Salsa Trio
- Bacon-Wrapped Shrimp
- Chicken Tenders with Dipping Sauces

Crispy Chicken Wings

Ingredients

- 12 chicken wings
- 2 tbsp olive oil
- 1 tsp garlic powder
- 1 tsp paprika
- Salt and pepper to taste
- Your favorite wing sauce (Buffalo, BBQ, etc.)

Instructions

1. Preheat your oven to 400°F (200°C).
2. Toss the chicken wings with olive oil, garlic powder, paprika, salt, and pepper.
3. Arrange the wings in a single layer on a baking sheet.
4. Bake for 25-30 minutes, flipping halfway through, until crispy and golden.
5. Toss in your favorite wing sauce and serve hot.

Mini Beef Sliders

Ingredients

- 1 lb ground beef
- 1/2 cup finely chopped onions
- Salt and pepper to taste
- Mini slider buns
- Cheese slices (optional)
- Pickles, lettuce, and condiments for topping

Instructions

1. Preheat a grill or skillet over medium heat.
2. Season the ground beef with salt and pepper, then form into small patties.
3. Grill or cook the patties for 3-4 minutes per side until cooked through.
4. Toast the slider buns lightly.
5. Assemble the sliders with the cooked patties, cheese, pickles, lettuce, and condiments.
6. Serve with a side of fries or chips.

Loaded Nachos

Ingredients

- Tortilla chips
- 1 cup shredded cheese (cheddar or Mexican blend)
- 1/2 cup black beans, drained and rinsed
- 1/4 cup sliced jalapeños
- 1/4 cup diced tomatoes
- 1/4 cup sour cream
- Guacamole (optional)
- Fresh cilantro for garnish

Instructions

1. Preheat the oven to 375°F (190°C).
2. Spread tortilla chips evenly on a baking sheet.
3. Top with cheese, black beans, jalapeños, and diced tomatoes.
4. Bake for 10-12 minutes until the cheese is melted and bubbly.
5. Remove from the oven and top with sour cream, guacamole, and cilantro.
6. Serve immediately and enjoy!

Classic Deviled Eggs

Ingredients

- 6 hard-boiled eggs, peeled and halved
- 2 tbsp mayonnaise
- 1 tsp mustard
- 1/4 tsp paprika
- Salt and pepper to taste
- Chopped chives or parsley for garnish

Instructions

1. Cut the hard-boiled eggs in half and remove the yolks.
2. Mash the yolks with mayonnaise, mustard, paprika, salt, and pepper.
3. Spoon or pipe the mixture back into the egg whites.
4. Garnish with chopped chives or parsley.
5. Serve chilled.

Veggie Spring Rolls

Ingredients

- Rice paper wrappers
- 1 cup shredded carrots
- 1/2 cup sliced cucumber
- 1/2 cup avocado slices
- Fresh mint and cilantro leaves
- 1/4 cup cooked rice noodles (optional)
- Soy sauce or peanut dipping sauce

Instructions

1. Soak rice paper wrappers in warm water until soft and pliable.
2. Lay the wrappers flat on a clean surface.
3. Place a small amount of shredded carrots, cucumber, avocado, mint, cilantro, and noodles (if using) in the center.
4. Roll the wrappers tightly, folding in the sides as you go.
5. Serve with soy sauce or peanut dipping sauce.

Stuffed Mushrooms

Ingredients

- 12 large mushroom caps
- 1/2 cup cream cheese, softened
- 1/4 cup grated Parmesan cheese
- 2 cloves garlic, minced
- 1/4 cup breadcrumbs
- Salt and pepper to taste

Instructions

1. Preheat the oven to 375°F (190°C).
2. Remove the stems from the mushroom caps and set them aside.
3. In a bowl, combine cream cheese, Parmesan, garlic, breadcrumbs, salt, and pepper.
4. Stuff the mushroom caps with the mixture.
5. Place the stuffed mushrooms on a baking sheet and bake for 15-20 minutes until golden and bubbly.
6. Serve warm.

Guacamole and Chips

Ingredients

- 3 ripe avocados, peeled and pitted
- 1/4 cup finely chopped onion
- 1 small tomato, diced
- 1 jalapeño, finely chopped (optional)
- 1 tbsp lime juice
- Salt and pepper to taste
- Tortilla chips for serving

Instructions

1. In a bowl, mash the avocados with a fork.
2. Add onion, tomato, jalapeño (if using), lime juice, salt, and pepper.
3. Stir to combine and adjust seasoning if needed.
4. Serve with tortilla chips.

Spinach and Artichoke Dip

Ingredients

- 1 cup frozen spinach, thawed and drained
- 1 cup canned artichoke hearts, drained and chopped
- 1/2 cup cream cheese, softened
- 1/4 cup sour cream
- 1/4 cup grated Parmesan cheese
- 1/2 cup shredded mozzarella cheese
- 1/4 tsp garlic powder
- Salt and pepper to taste

Instructions

1. Preheat the oven to 375°F (190°C).
2. In a bowl, combine spinach, artichokes, cream cheese, sour cream, Parmesan, mozzarella, garlic powder, salt, and pepper.
3. Transfer the mixture to a baking dish and smooth the top.
4. Bake for 20-25 minutes until bubbly and golden on top.
5. Serve warm with pita chips or crackers.

Meatball Sliders

Ingredients

- 12 small meatballs (store-bought or homemade)
- 12 slider buns
- 1 cup marinara sauce
- 1/2 cup mozzarella cheese, shredded
- Fresh basil for garnish (optional)

Instructions

1. Heat the meatballs in marinara sauce on the stove or in the oven until hot.
2. Toast the slider buns lightly.
3. Place one meatball on each bun, top with marinara sauce and mozzarella cheese.
4. Serve warm and garnish with fresh basil if desired.

Caprese Skewers

Ingredients

- Cherry tomatoes
- Fresh mozzarella balls
- Fresh basil leaves
- Balsamic glaze
- Salt and pepper to taste

Instructions

1. Thread a cherry tomato, a mozzarella ball, and a basil leaf onto small skewers or toothpicks.
2. Arrange the skewers on a serving platter.
3. Drizzle with balsamic glaze and season with salt and pepper.
4. Serve chilled or at room temperature.

Buffalo Cauliflower Bites

Ingredients

- 1 head cauliflower, cut into florets
- 1 cup flour
- 1/2 cup water
- 1 tsp garlic powder
- 1 tsp paprika
- 1/2 cup buffalo sauce
- 1 tbsp olive oil
- Ranch dressing for dipping

Instructions

1. Preheat the oven to 400°F (200°C).
2. In a bowl, whisk together flour, water, garlic powder, and paprika until smooth.
3. Dip the cauliflower florets into the batter and arrange them on a baking sheet.
4. Bake for 20-25 minutes until crispy and golden.
5. Toss the baked cauliflower in buffalo sauce and return to the oven for another 5-10 minutes.
6. Serve with ranch dressing.

Shrimp Cocktail

Ingredients

- 1 lb cooked shrimp, peeled and deveined
- 1 cup cocktail sauce
- Lemon wedges for garnish

Instructions

1. Arrange the cooked shrimp on a platter around a bowl of cocktail sauce.
2. Garnish with lemon wedges.
3. Serve chilled.

Cheese and Charcuterie Board

Ingredients

- Assorted cheeses (brie, cheddar, goat cheese, etc.)
- Assorted meats (prosciutto, salami, etc.)
- Olives, pickles, and nuts
- Fresh fruits (grapes, apple slices, etc.)
- Crackers or baguette slices

Instructions

1. Arrange the cheeses, meats, olives, and fruits on a large board or platter.
2. Fill in the gaps with crackers and nuts.
3. Serve with a selection of wine or other beverages.

Pigs in a Blanket

Ingredients

- 1 package mini cocktail sausages
- 1 package crescent roll dough
- Mustard or ketchup for dipping

Instructions

1. Preheat the oven to 375°F (190°C).
2. Unroll the crescent dough and cut it into small strips.
3. Wrap each cocktail sausage with a strip of dough and place on a baking sheet.
4. Bake for 10-12 minutes or until golden brown.
5. Serve with mustard or ketchup for dipping.

Baked Brie with Jam

Ingredients

- 1 wheel of brie cheese
- 1/4 cup fruit jam (apricot or raspberry works well)
- Fresh herbs (rosemary or thyme)
- Crackers or sliced baguette

Instructions

1. Preheat the oven to 350°F (175°C).
2. Place the brie on a baking sheet and top with jam.
3. Bake for 10-12 minutes until the cheese is soft and gooey.
4. Garnish with fresh herbs and serve with crackers or sliced baguette.

Mini Quiches

Ingredients

- 1 sheet puff pastry
- 3 large eggs
- 1/2 cup heavy cream
- 1/4 cup grated cheese (cheddar, Swiss, or feta)
- 1/4 cup cooked spinach, chopped
- Salt and pepper to taste

Instructions

1. Preheat the oven to 375°F (190°C).
2. Roll out the puff pastry and cut into small circles to fit into a muffin tin.
3. In a bowl, whisk together eggs, heavy cream, cheese, spinach, salt, and pepper.
4. Pour the mixture into the pastry-lined muffin tin.
5. Bake for 15-18 minutes until the quiches are set and lightly golden.

Hummus with Pita and Veggies

Ingredients

- 1 cup hummus (store-bought or homemade)
- 1 pita bread, cut into wedges
- **Carrot sticks, cucumber slices, and bell pepper strips**

Instructions

1. Arrange the hummus in the center of a serving platter.
2. Arrange the pita wedges and vegetables around the hummus.
3. Serve as a healthy and refreshing appetizer.

Guacamole-Stuffed Peppers

Ingredients

- Mini bell peppers, halved and seeded
- 1 ripe avocado, mashed
- 1 tbsp lime juice
- 1/4 cup diced tomato
- 1/4 cup chopped cilantro
- Salt and pepper to taste

Instructions

1. Mix the mashed avocado, lime juice, tomato, cilantro, salt, and pepper in a bowl.
2. Stuff the mini bell pepper halves with the guacamole mixture.
3. Serve immediately for a fresh, bite-sized treat.

Bacon-Wrapped Dates

Ingredients

- 12 dates, pitted
- 12 slices of bacon
- **Toothpicks for securing**

Instructions

1. Preheat the oven to 400°F (200°C).
2. Wrap each date with a slice of bacon and secure with a toothpick.
3. Place on a baking sheet and bake for 15-20 minutes until the bacon is crispy.
4. Serve warm and enjoy the sweet and savory combination.

Jalapeño Poppers

Ingredients

- 12 jalapeño peppers, halved and seeded
- 4 oz cream cheese, softened
- 1/4 cup shredded cheddar cheese
- 1/4 cup cooked bacon, crumbled
- 1/4 tsp garlic powder
- 1/4 tsp paprika
- Salt and pepper to taste

Instructions

1. Preheat the oven to 375°F (190°C).
2. Mix the cream cheese, cheddar cheese, bacon, garlic powder, paprika, salt, and pepper in a bowl.
3. Stuff each jalapeño half with the cheese mixture.
4. Place on a baking sheet and bake for 15-20 minutes until the peppers are tender and the cheese is melted.
5. Serve hot.

Chicken Satay with Peanut Sauce

Ingredients

- 1 lb chicken breast, cut into strips
- 1/4 cup soy sauce
- 2 tbsp peanut butter
- 2 tbsp honey
- 1 tbsp lime juice
- 1 tsp garlic powder
- 1 tsp ginger powder
- Wooden skewers (soaked in water)

Instructions

1. In a bowl, mix soy sauce, peanut butter, honey, lime juice, garlic, and ginger.
2. Thread the chicken strips onto wooden skewers and marinate in the peanut sauce for at least 30 minutes.
3. Preheat the grill or grill pan over medium heat.
4. Grill the chicken skewers for 4-5 minutes per side until cooked through.
5. Serve with extra peanut sauce for dipping.

Spinach and Cheese Stuffed Pretzels

Ingredients

- 1 package pizza dough
- 1 cup spinach, chopped
- 1/2 cup ricotta cheese
- 1/4 cup mozzarella cheese, shredded
- 1 tbsp olive oil
- 1/2 tsp garlic powder
- Coarse salt for sprinkling

Instructions

1. Preheat the oven to 375°F (190°C).
2. Roll out the pizza dough and cut it into small squares.
3. Mix spinach, ricotta, mozzarella, olive oil, and garlic powder in a bowl.
4. Place a spoonful of the spinach mixture in the center of each dough square.
5. Fold the dough over the filling and twist to form a pretzel shape.
6. Place on a baking sheet, sprinkle with coarse salt, and bake for 15-18 minutes until golden brown.

Shrimp and Avocado Crostini

Ingredients

- 1 baguette, sliced
- 1 lb shrimp, peeled and deveined
- 1 avocado, mashed
- 1 tbsp lime juice
- 1 tbsp olive oil
- Salt and pepper to taste
- Chopped cilantro for garnish

Instructions

1. Toast the baguette slices in the oven at 375°F (190°C) for 8-10 minutes until crisp.
2. Sauté the shrimp in olive oil for 2-3 minutes until pink and cooked through.
3. Mash the avocado with lime juice, salt, and pepper.
4. Spread the mashed avocado on each crostini.
5. Top with a shrimp and garnish with cilantro.

Mini Tacos

Ingredients

- 1 lb ground beef or chicken
- 1 tbsp taco seasoning
- Mini taco shells
- 1/2 cup shredded lettuce
- 1/4 cup diced tomatoes
- 1/4 cup shredded cheese
- Sour cream and salsa for topping

Instructions

1. Cook the ground beef or chicken in a skillet over medium heat until browned.
2. Add taco seasoning and follow package instructions.
3. Warm the mini taco shells in the oven.
4. Assemble the tacos by adding a spoonful of meat, lettuce, tomatoes, and cheese.
5. Serve with sour cream and salsa on the side.

Cheese-Stuffed Breadsticks

Ingredients

- 1 package pizza dough
- 1 cup mozzarella cheese, shredded
- 1/2 cup Parmesan cheese, grated
- 1 tbsp garlic butter
- Dipping sauce (marinara or ranch)

Instructions

1. Preheat the oven to 375°F (190°C).
2. Roll out the pizza dough into a rectangle.
3. Sprinkle mozzarella and Parmesan cheese over half of the dough.
4. Fold the dough over and press to seal the edges.
5. Cut the dough into strips and twist them.
6. Bake for 10-12 minutes until golden brown.
7. Brush with garlic butter and serve with dipping sauce.

Sweet and Sour Meatballs

Ingredients

- 1 lb ground beef or pork
- 1/2 cup breadcrumbs
- 1 egg
- 1/4 cup onion, finely chopped
- 1/4 cup ketchup
- 1/4 cup brown sugar
- 1/4 cup vinegar
- 1/4 cup soy sauce
- 1 tbsp cornstarch

Instructions

1. Preheat the oven to 375°F (190°C).
2. Mix ground meat, breadcrumbs, egg, and onion. Roll into small meatballs.
3. Place meatballs on a baking sheet and bake for 20 minutes.
4. In a saucepan, mix ketchup, brown sugar, vinegar, soy sauce, and cornstarch.
5. Bring the sauce to a simmer and cook until thickened.
6. Toss the meatballs in the sweet and sour sauce and serve.

Bruschetta with Tomato and Basil

Ingredients

- 1 baguette, sliced
- 2 cups tomatoes, diced
- 1/4 cup fresh basil, chopped
- 2 tbsp olive oil
- 1 tbsp balsamic vinegar
- Garlic clove, peeled
- Salt and pepper to taste

Instructions

1. Toast the baguette slices in the oven at 375°F (190°C) for 8-10 minutes.
2. Rub each toast with a cut garlic clove for extra flavor.
3. Mix tomatoes, basil, olive oil, balsamic vinegar, salt, and pepper in a bowl.
4. Spoon the mixture onto the toasted bread and serve immediately.

Mozzarella Sticks

Ingredients

- 1 lb mozzarella cheese, cut into sticks
- 1 cup flour
- 2 eggs, beaten
- 1 cup breadcrumbs
- 1/2 tsp garlic powder
- Oil for frying
- Marinara sauce for dipping

Instructions

1. Dredge the mozzarella sticks in flour, then dip in beaten eggs, and coat in breadcrumbs mixed with garlic powder.
2. Freeze the coated sticks for at least 30 minutes.
3. Heat oil in a frying pan over medium heat.
4. Fry the mozzarella sticks for 1-2 minutes on each side until golden and crispy.
5. Serve with marinara sauce.

Sweet Potato Fries with Dip

Ingredients

- 2 large sweet potatoes, cut into fries
- 2 tbsp olive oil
- 1 tsp paprika
- Salt and pepper to taste
- 1/2 cup sour cream
- 1 tbsp ketchup
- 1 tbsp sriracha sauce

Instructions

1. Preheat the oven to 400°F (200°C).
2. Toss sweet potato fries in olive oil, paprika, salt, and pepper.
3. Arrange the fries in a single layer on a baking sheet and bake for 20-25 minutes until crispy.
4. Mix sour cream, ketchup, and sriracha sauce to make the dip.
5. Serve the fries with the dipping sauce.

Mini Caprese Bites

Ingredients

- Cherry tomatoes, halved
- Fresh mozzarella balls (bocconcini)
- Fresh basil leaves
- Balsamic glaze
- Toothpicks

Instructions

1. Skewer a cherry tomato half, followed by a mozzarella ball, and then a fresh basil leaf onto a toothpick.
2. Arrange on a platter and drizzle with balsamic glaze before serving.

Loaded Potato Skins

Ingredients

- 4 large russet potatoes
- 1/2 cup sour cream
- 1/2 cup shredded cheddar cheese
- 4 slices cooked bacon, crumbled
- 2 green onions, chopped
- Olive oil
- Salt and pepper to taste

Instructions

1. Preheat the oven to 400°F (200°C).
2. Wash and bake potatoes for about 45 minutes or until tender.
3. Let the potatoes cool slightly, then slice them in half and scoop out the flesh, leaving about 1/4 inch of potato in the skins.
4. Brush the skins with olive oil and bake again for 10-15 minutes until crispy.
5. Fill the skins with sour cream, cheese, bacon, and green onions, and bake for another 5 minutes to melt the cheese.
6. Serve immediately.

Stuffed Jalapeños

Ingredients

- 10 fresh jalapeños, halved and seeded
- 8 oz cream cheese, softened
- 1/2 cup shredded cheddar cheese
- 1/4 cup breadcrumbs
- 1 tbsp olive oil
- 1/2 tsp garlic powder
- Salt and pepper to taste

Instructions

1. Preheat the oven to 375°F (190°C).
2. Mix cream cheese, cheddar cheese, breadcrumbs, garlic powder, salt, and pepper.
3. Fill each jalapeño half with the cream cheese mixture.
4. Drizzle with olive oil and bake for 20-25 minutes until golden and bubbly.
5. Serve warm.

Cucumber Bites with Cream Cheese

Ingredients

- 1 cucumber, sliced
- 8 oz cream cheese, softened
- 1 tbsp fresh dill, chopped
- 1 tbsp lemon juice
- Salt and pepper to taste

Instructions

1. In a bowl, mix cream cheese, dill, lemon juice, salt, and pepper.
2. Spread a small amount of the cream cheese mixture onto each cucumber slice.
3. Garnish with additional dill if desired and serve immediately.

Pulled Pork Sliders

Ingredients

- 2 cups pulled pork (cooked and shredded)
- 8 slider buns
- 1/2 cup BBQ sauce
- Pickles (optional)

Instructions

1. Mix pulled pork with BBQ sauce.
2. Spoon the pulled pork onto slider buns and top with pickles if desired.
3. Serve immediately for a delicious and easy appetizer.

Veggie Platter with Dip

Ingredients

- **Assorted fresh veggies (carrot sticks, cucumber slices, cherry tomatoes, bell pepper strips, etc.)**
- **1 cup hummus or ranch dip**

Instructions

1. Arrange the veggies in an attractive pattern on a platter.
2. Serve with a side of hummus or ranch dip for dipping.

Meat and Cheese Empanadas

Ingredients

- 1 package empanada dough discs
- 1/2 lb ground beef
- 1/2 onion, chopped
- 1/2 cup shredded cheddar cheese
- 1/2 tsp cumin
- Salt and pepper to taste
- 1 egg, beaten (for egg wash)

Instructions

1. Preheat the oven to 375°F (190°C).
2. Brown the ground beef with onions in a skillet, seasoning with cumin, salt, and pepper.
3. Let the beef mixture cool slightly before placing a spoonful of it onto each empanada dough disc.
4. Add some shredded cheese on top and fold the dough over to seal the empanada.
5. Brush with egg wash and bake for 20-25 minutes until golden.
6. Serve warm.

Popcorn Chicken

Ingredients

- 2 cups chicken breast, cut into small bite-sized pieces
- 1 cup buttermilk
- 1 1/2 cups breadcrumbs
- 1/2 tsp garlic powder
- 1/2 tsp paprika
- Salt and pepper to taste
- Oil for frying

Instructions

1. Marinate the chicken pieces in buttermilk for at least 30 minutes.
2. In a bowl, mix breadcrumbs with garlic powder, paprika, salt, and pepper.
3. Dredge the marinated chicken in the breadcrumb mixture.
4. Heat oil in a pan over medium heat and fry the chicken for 3-4 minutes until golden and crispy.
5. Serve with your favorite dipping sauce.

Fruit and Cheese Skewers

Ingredients

- 1 cup cubed cheddar cheese
- 1 cup cubed brie cheese
- Assorted fresh fruit (grapes, strawberries, pineapple, etc.)
- Wooden skewers

Instructions

1. Alternate threading pieces of cheese and fruit onto wooden skewers.
2. Arrange on a platter and serve chilled or at room temperature.

Shrimp Spring Rolls

Ingredients

- 1/2 lb cooked shrimp, peeled and deveined
- 8-10 rice paper wrappers
- 1 cup lettuce leaves, shredded
- 1/2 cucumber, julienned
- 1 carrot, julienned
- Fresh cilantro leaves
- 1/4 cup hoisin sauce
- 1/4 cup peanut butter (optional for dipping sauce)
- Lime wedges (for serving)

Instructions

1. Prepare the rice paper wrappers by soaking them one at a time in warm water for about 10-15 seconds until soft.
2. Lay the softened wrapper on a flat surface and layer shrimp, lettuce, cucumber, carrot, and cilantro in the center.
3. Fold the sides of the wrapper over the filling and roll tightly.
4. Repeat for the remaining ingredients.
5. For dipping sauce, mix hoisin sauce and peanut butter if desired, and serve with lime wedges.

Cheddar and Bacon Biscuits

Ingredients

- 2 cups all-purpose flour
- 1 tbsp baking powder
- 1/2 tsp salt
- 1/4 tsp garlic powder
- 1/2 cup cold unsalted butter, cubed
- 3/4 cup shredded cheddar cheese
- 1/4 cup cooked bacon, crumbled
- 1/2 cup whole milk
- 1 egg (for egg wash)

Instructions

1. Preheat the oven to 400°F (200°C).
2. In a bowl, combine flour, baking powder, salt, and garlic powder.
3. Cut the cold butter into the dry ingredients using a pastry cutter or your fingers until the mixture resembles coarse crumbs.
4. Stir in the cheese and bacon.
5. Gradually add milk and mix until just combined.
6. Turn dough onto a floured surface, knead gently, and roll it out to about 1-inch thickness.
7. Cut biscuits using a round cutter and place them on a baking sheet.
8. Brush the tops with egg wash and bake for 12-15 minutes, or until golden.

Parmesan Zucchini Fries

Ingredients

- 2 medium zucchinis, sliced into sticks
- 1/2 cup breadcrumbs
- 1/2 cup grated Parmesan cheese
- 1/2 tsp garlic powder
- Salt and pepper to taste
- 1 egg, beaten
- Olive oil for drizzling

Instructions

1. Preheat the oven to 425°F (220°C).
2. In a shallow bowl, combine breadcrumbs, Parmesan, garlic powder, salt, and pepper.
3. Dip zucchini sticks into the beaten egg, then coat them with the breadcrumb mixture.
4. Place the coated zucchini sticks on a baking sheet lined with parchment paper.
5. Drizzle with olive oil and bake for 15-20 minutes, flipping halfway, until golden and crispy.
6. Serve with marinara sauce for dipping.

Tzatziki with Fresh Veggies

Ingredients

- 1 cup Greek yogurt
- 1/2 cucumber, grated and excess water squeezed out
- 1 tbsp olive oil
- 1 tbsp fresh dill, chopped
- 1 tbsp lemon juice
- 1 garlic clove, minced
- Salt and pepper to taste
- Assorted fresh veggies (carrot sticks, cucumber slices, bell peppers, etc.)

Instructions

1. In a bowl, combine yogurt, grated cucumber, olive oil, dill, lemon juice, garlic, salt, and pepper.
2. Mix well and refrigerate for at least 30 minutes to allow the flavors to meld.
3. Serve with fresh veggies for dipping.

Beef Empanadas

Ingredients

- 1 lb ground beef
- 1/2 onion, finely chopped
- 1/2 tsp cumin
- 1/2 tsp paprika
- Salt and pepper to taste
- 1 package empanada dough discs
- 1 egg, beaten (for egg wash)

Instructions

1. In a skillet, brown the ground beef and onion over medium heat.
2. Add cumin, paprika, salt, and pepper, and cook for another 5 minutes until well combined.
3. Let the beef mixture cool slightly.
4. Spoon a small amount of the beef mixture onto each empanada dough disc, fold over, and press to seal the edges.
5. Brush with egg wash and bake at 375°F (190°C) for 20-25 minutes until golden brown.
6. Serve warm.

Taco Dip

Ingredients

- 1 package cream cheese, softened
- 1/2 cup sour cream
- 1 packet taco seasoning mix
- 1 cup salsa
- 1 cup shredded cheddar cheese
- 1/2 cup green onions, chopped
- 1/2 cup black olives, sliced

Instructions

1. In a bowl, combine cream cheese, sour cream, and taco seasoning, mixing until smooth.
2. Spread the mixture in the bottom of a serving dish.
3. Top with salsa, shredded cheddar, green onions, and black olives.
4. Serve with tortilla chips or fresh veggies for dipping.

Bruschetta with Goat Cheese

Ingredients

- 1 baguette, sliced into 1-inch pieces
- 4 oz goat cheese, softened
- 1 cup cherry tomatoes, diced
- 1/4 cup fresh basil, chopped
- 2 tbsp balsamic glaze
- Salt and pepper to taste

Instructions

1. Preheat the oven to 375°F (190°C).
2. Place the baguette slices on a baking sheet and toast in the oven for 5-7 minutes, until golden and crispy.
3. In a small bowl, combine the goat cheese with a pinch of salt and pepper.
4. Spread a generous layer of goat cheese on each toasted baguette slice.
5. In another bowl, mix the diced tomatoes and basil, then spoon onto the goat cheese.
6. Drizzle with balsamic glaze and serve immediately.

Caprese Salad Bites

Ingredients

- 1 pint cherry tomatoes
- 8 oz fresh mozzarella balls (bocconcini or ciliegine)
- Fresh basil leaves
- Balsamic glaze
- Olive oil for drizzling
- Salt and pepper to taste

Instructions

1. Thread one cherry tomato, one mozzarella ball, and one basil leaf onto small skewers or toothpicks.
2. Arrange the skewers on a platter.
3. Drizzle with olive oil and balsamic glaze.
4. Sprinkle with salt and pepper to taste.
5. Serve chilled or at room temperature.

Crab Cakes with Remoulade

Ingredients

- 1 lb crab meat (fresh or canned, drained)
- 1/2 cup breadcrumbs
- 1/4 cup mayonnaise
- 1 egg
- 1 tbsp Dijon mustard
- 1 tbsp lemon juice
- 1/4 cup green onions, chopped
- 1/4 tsp Old Bay seasoning
- Salt and pepper to taste
- Olive oil for frying

Remoulade Sauce Ingredients

- 1/2 cup mayonnaise
- 1 tbsp Dijon mustard
- 1 tbsp lemon juice
- 1 tbsp capers, chopped
- 1 tsp hot sauce
- 1/2 tsp paprika
- Salt and pepper to taste

Instructions

1. In a bowl, combine crab meat, breadcrumbs, mayonnaise, egg, Dijon mustard, lemon juice, green onions, Old Bay seasoning, salt, and pepper.
2. Shape the mixture into small patties.
3. Heat olive oil in a skillet over medium heat and fry the crab cakes for about 3-4 minutes on each side, until golden brown.
4. For the remoulade sauce, mix all ingredients in a bowl.
5. Serve the crab cakes with a side of remoulade sauce for dipping.

Guacamole and Salsa Trio

Ingredients

- 1 large ripe avocado, mashed
- 1/4 cup red onion, finely chopped
- 1 tbsp lime juice
- 1 tbsp cilantro, chopped
- Salt to taste

Salsa 1: Classic Tomato Salsa

- 2 medium tomatoes, diced
- 1/4 cup red onion, chopped
- 1 tbsp cilantro, chopped
- 1 jalapeño, minced
- 1 tbsp lime juice
- Salt to taste

Salsa 2: Mango Salsa

- 1 mango, peeled and diced
- 1/4 cup red bell pepper, diced
- 1/4 cup red onion, finely chopped
- 1 tbsp cilantro, chopped
- 1 tbsp lime juice
- Salt to taste

Instructions

1. For the guacamole, mash the avocado in a bowl and mix with red onion, lime juice, cilantro, and salt.
2. For the tomato salsa, combine all the salsa ingredients in a bowl and mix well.
3. For the mango salsa, combine all the salsa ingredients and toss to combine.
4. Serve the guacamole with tortilla chips and the salsas as a trio.

Bacon-Wrapped Shrimp

Ingredients

- 12 large shrimp, peeled and deveined
- 6 slices bacon, cut in half
- 1 tbsp olive oil
- 1 tbsp lemon juice
- 1/4 tsp smoked paprika
- Salt and pepper to taste

Instructions

1. Preheat the oven to 400°F (200°C).
2. Wrap each shrimp with a half slice of bacon and secure with a toothpick.
3. Place the bacon-wrapped shrimp on a baking sheet.
4. Drizzle with olive oil, lemon juice, smoked paprika, salt, and pepper.
5. Bake for 12-15 minutes, or until the bacon is crispy and the shrimp are cooked through.
6. Serve immediately.

Chicken Tenders with Dipping Sauces

Ingredients

- 1 lb chicken tenders
- 1 cup flour
- 1 tsp garlic powder
- 1 tsp paprika
- 1/2 tsp salt
- 1/2 tsp pepper
- 2 eggs, beaten
- 1 cup breadcrumbs
- Olive oil for frying

Dipping Sauces

- Honey mustard
- Barbecue sauce
- Ranch dressing

Instructions

1. In a bowl, mix flour, garlic powder, paprika, salt, and pepper.
2. Dip each chicken tender first into the flour mixture, then into the beaten eggs, and finally coat with breadcrumbs.
3. Heat olive oil in a skillet over medium heat and fry the chicken tenders for about 4-5 minutes on each side until golden brown.
4. Serve with honey mustard, barbecue sauce, and ranch dressing for dipping.

www.ingramcontent.com/pod-product-compliance
Lightning Source LLC
LaVergne TN
LVHW081342060526
838201LV00055B/2813